Keeping School Cool!

A Kid's Guide to Handling School Problems

Written by
Michaelene Mundy

Illustrated by
R. W. Alley

ABBEY PRESS

Publications
St. Meinrad, IN 47577

Many thanks to Emily and Andrew,
who were my consultants in recalling school problems
and the feelings associated with them.
As high school students, they were closer to those
elementary fears and concerns than I.

Text © 2002 Michaelene Mundy
Illustrations © 2002 St. Meinrad Archabbey
Published by Abbey Press Publications
1 Hill Drive
St. Meinrad, Indiana 47577

Library of Congress Catalog Number
2001095355

ISBN 978-0-87029-359-7

Printed in the United States of America.

A Message to Parents, Teachers, and Other Caring Adults

From the end of August until the first part of June, children spend many more hours at school than their waking hours at home. For seven or eight hours a day, they must "fend for themselves," away from the protective arms and eyes of parents. They deal with people of all ages—on the bus, in class, at lunch and recess. They learn many social skills through trial and error.

Adults must take care not to belittle a child's concerns about school. These problems may seem trivial compared to adult worries, but a child's problems can be just as gut-wrenching and nerve-wracking. When a child comes home from school, it's important that someone show an interest in how the day went.

A good starting place is your child's backpack. You can unearth treasures to display with pride on the refrigerator and then tuck away in a memory box. That backpack also contains many "conversation starters"—corrected papers, test grades, updates and notes from the teacher.

Even though teachers and bus drivers try to be aware of what's going on, they are not omniscient. Cliques, conflicts, and bullying do happen. Try to get your child to talk about problems like this, and come up with a plan of action. If a child has been hurt or threatened with harm, of course, you need to alert school authorities.

We cannot always protect our children from daily hardships, however, and we shouldn't. A child doesn't learn responsibility, for example, if a parent rushes to school with homework inadvertently left on the kitchen table. It's up to adults to find a good balance between intervening and allowing a child to deal with his or her own difficulties.

I hope this book will help you to pinpoint any problems your child may be having, so that you can offer the perspective, reassurance, or extra help needed to keep school cool!

—*Michaelene Mundy*

The First Day

The first day of school is exciting! You may have new clothes to wear. You might have new things—like a fresh box of crayons and a full bottle of glue that isn't all gunked up at the spout.

The first day of school can be scary, too. You have a new teacher, a new classroom, and new books. You may know some classmates, but not others.

Most of your classmates feel just as you do—excited and scared at the same time. As you get used to things in the next few days, it won't feel so scary anymore.

Learning Takes Time

When you flip through the pages of your new books, you may find some words or problems that look hard. Don't worry! Your teacher will explain all this later in the year. You will learn new things little by little.

If you're having trouble learning something, keep trying. Ask your teacher for help after class, or take your book home to practice. Be sure to let your parents and teacher know if you still can't get it.

Your teacher knows how to tell if you have what is called a "learning problem." She can make sure that you get special help, so you don't get behind in your work.

So Much to Do

Kids have a lot to do! You go to school all day. Then you might have soccer practice, piano lessons, and lots of homework.

If you feel worried about all you have to do, you may need to change the way you do some things. Try to start ahead of time to study for a test or to do a project. If you get time in school to do homework, make good use of that time.

Be sure to eat healthy food to keep your mind and body working well. When you can't eat supper till late because you have practice, ask Mom or Dad to bring you a sandwich and some juice.

Tips on Teachers

If you don't understand something in class, raise your hand and ask a question. There are no stupid questions. You may be asking the same thing another student was too shy to ask.

If you don't know why something was marked wrong on a paper, ask your teacher to explain it.

Sometimes kids think their teacher doesn't like them. If you're having teacher trouble, talk with your parents about it. They can set up a time for all of you to sit down together with your teacher and work out the problem.

Homework Helps

School and homework go together like sports and practice. Homework helps you practice your school skills. It lets the teacher know what you understand and what you need to work on.

Don't worry if you make some mistakes on your homework. Mistakes are part of learning. When you go over your paper later, you can find out what you did wrong. Then you can get it right the next time!

It helps to have a special place for homework. You need a desk or table to write on and spread out your things. You need a quiet place, away from the TV, video game, or loud music.

It may help if a parent is near, in case you have a question. But, remember, it is your homework. It won't help you learn if someone else does the work.

Making Friends

You can't "make" friends the way you make a clay animal or a house out of blocks. You make friends by getting to know them, helping them, inviting them to play with you. To make a friend, you must be a friend.

Sometimes one friend may think you aren't her friend anymore if you have other friends. Help her to understand that she is still your friend, and all of you can play together. You can have lots of "best" friends.

Try to be kind to everyone, even those who aren't your best friends. When you look for the best in people, you help people to be their best.

Feeling Left Out

Team captains usually choose their friends or the best players first. If you are one of the last to be chosen, you might feel hurt and left out.

Maybe you aren't the fastest runner, but you have a good, loud voice to cheer on your team. Play and have fun. That's more important than winning anyway!

Feeling "different" can also make you feel left out. Know what? You *are* different. Everyone else is different, too! Wouldn't it be a boring world if we all looked the same, liked the same things, and had the same talents? We have so much to learn from each other!

Getting in Trouble

Everyone gets into trouble at school sometime. You might be talking in class instead of listening. Or maybe you forgot to do your homework.

When you act up in class, or don't do your work, it isn't fair. It's not fair to your teacher, who is trying to help a lot of kids learn. It's not fair to your classmates, because you are keeping them from learning. It's not fair to *you*, because you're losing out on learning too!

If you get in trouble, take time to think about what you did wrong. Tell your teacher you're sorry, and try hard not to do it again.

Feeling Sick

What if you wake up with a stomachache? Your mom and dad will decide whether you need to stay home or go to school.

They might ask if you are worried about something, like a test. When you are worried, it can give you a stomachache. Once you talk about what is bothering you, often you will feel better.

If you feel sick at school, tell your teacher. He will probably send you to the school nurse. The nurse may let you lie down awhile to see if you feel better. She knows how to get in touch with your mom or dad if you need to go home.

Learning Is Fun

One of the hardest things about school is paying attention the whole time. It's easy to feel like talking or moving around when you're not supposed to. But if you're really interested in what you're doing, it's much easier to pay attention.

Many classes have a "Show and Tell" time. You can learn about your classmates' rock or baseball card collections. You can bring pictures of your pet gerbil to share with the class.

Your mind is like a sponge that never gets filled up. Soak up all the new facts and ideas you can. School is cool when your mind is wide open to learn and share!

Teamwork and Schoolwork

Good manners are always a good idea, especially at school. Remember to say "Please" and "Thank you" to your classmates, teacher, and the cafeteria workers.

Sometimes you may get to work with other kids on a lesson or project. Be sure to do your part—but don't do it all yourself! Listen to others' ideas and work together as a team.

It's not a good idea to let a friend "copy" your paper when you are not working together in a group. It's hard to tell a friend no, but this is cheating. Each of you needs to do your own work in order to learn.

Safe at School

People who tease or hurt others on purpose are called "bullies." Bullies try to look smarter, stronger, or more important by picking on others.

If you don't like the way someone is treating you, just walk away. Fighting or yelling at a bully doesn't do any good. If someone keeps on bothering you, tell a teacher.

Sometimes kids who are very angry inside might talk about hurting people or the school. They may think it's "funny" or makes them seem tough. Or they may really plan on doing something harmful.

If you ever hear any talk like this, tell a grown-up right away. Kids like this need special help, so they can handle their feelings in a better way.

Solving Problems

There are many people who care about you and want you to do well in school. If you have any kind of problem at all, ask for help.

You can go to a teacher, counselor, nurse, secretary, or the principal. You can talk with your parents, or an older brother or sister.

If someone tells you that your problem is no big deal, let him or her know it's important to you. Sometimes older kids or grown-ups can forget how hard it is to learn so many new things every day.

The Success Express

"School" is not just learning from books and doing papers. It is getting to know people and doing things together. It is exploring the world around us—and how the world used to be or might be in the future.

Someday you'll look back and see how school helped you do things and get to places you never thought you could go.

If you want to go far in life, school can be the express to a life of success!

Michaelene Mundy holds degrees in elementary education, as well as graduate degrees in school and community counseling. She has taught third and fourth graders, worked with learning-disabled children, and has served as a counselor on the college level. The mother of three children, she now works as a high school guidance counselor. She is also the author of three other Elf-help Books for Kids.

R. W. Alley is the illustrator for the popular Abbey Press adult series of Elf-help books, as well as an illustrator and writer of children's books. He lives in Barrington, Rhode Island, with his wife, daughter, and son. See a wide variety of his works at: www.rwalley.com.